1897767 005

Delectation Books -

a collaboration between

Delectus Books
27 Old Gloucester Street
London WC1N 3XX
(Tel: 081-963-0979)

- and -

Creation Press
83 Clerkenwell Road
London EC1M 5RJ
(Tel: 071-430-9878)

THE 120 DAYS OF SODOM

by
NICK HEDGES

Freely adapted from the novel
by the Marquis de Sade

PRESS COMMENT

"Two hundred years on, the dark and stenching imagination of the Marquis de Sade retains its power to appal"

- THE INDEPENDENT

"Nick Hedges' adaptation and production is undeniably clever in the way that it uses white faces, gender swapping, ritual and camp humour to undermine any possible eroticism in the content. Some of the material is simply puke-making, but most of it reveals that Sade was dealing with power just as much as sex. The four libertines get off on forcing their unwilling victims to suffer, in the same way that torturers do throughout the world. If for most people consent is the crucial issue, then Sade's establishment figures go way beyond this with their knuckledusters up the arse, branding, and flaying of skin which is afterwards seen to be delicately consumed. It makes for gruesome, disturbing viewing, and any audience titters are very much on the actors' own terms which says much for the power of Hedges' production"

- TIME OUT

"It has become fashionable to view Sade as a libertarian who freed sexuality from the shackles of conventional morality; whereas, as Nick Hedges' adaptation makes clear, he was a libertine whose coupling of pain and pleasure was the product of a confined body and a confused mind. Mr. Hedges has bravely chosen to dramatise a novel which it is almost impossible to describe in the pages of this newspaper. But this is no more an evening for those in dirty raincoats than it is for those with weak stomachs, for Mr. Hedges adopts a rigorously stylised approach. His cast wear white make-up, half way between th. mask of the mime and the pallor of the ancien regime. Sounds are amplified and juxtaposed, such as the turning of pages and scraping of knives, and movement is self-consciously slow. The overall effect - together with the billowing smoke, guttering candles and sacred music - is of a black mass ... Mr. Hedges' scheme makes perfect sense"

- EVENING STANDARD

"A bizarre pantomime of depravity that makes the Kama Sutra read like a guide to personal hygiene. This production pursues a caustic camp irony which lightens the tone, but leaves gnawingly disturbing images"

- WHAT'S ON

"Nick Hedges, adapter and director, demonstrates a sure theatrical skill in choosing excerpts from the Marquis de Sade's notorious work and fashioning these into a sequence of increasing sadism which steadily extends a mood that is at once giddying and desolate. The scene is made to seem still more hellish by the silence. Mouths open to shape a scream, but when there is a sound, which mostly there is not, it is disembodied and amplified. Often the cruelty is played against the sound of an infernal howling wind. Sometimes a dismemberment is indicated by a black ribbon tied around the wrist. Hedges has trained in Japanese theatre which uses similar effects, and the slow, dainty tread of the figures can be traced to the same source. To stage the book at all is some kind of achievement; likewise to create such a convincing sense of evil"

- THE TIMES

"Nick Hedges pulls powerful visual punches. The libertines' startling white faces are dashed blue-black, like bruises, around the eyes, and their mouths - coarse smears of red - open like flaccid sores. Beauty, meanwhile, counterpoises ugliness. A couple, decked in pale marriage veils and laurels of old gold, dance, softly lit by candles clasped in their abusers' hands. Elsewhere choristers and baroque harmonies, elegant as Sade's prose accompany atrocities"

- THE GUARDIAN

"A brilliant stylistic creation, from the whiplash page-turning to the Kellogg's Mini Variety packs"

- CITY LIMITS

"The production was certainly one De Sade would have approved of. Opulent and eccentric, it constantly hit home. This is an incitement to riot. The best of Lindsay Kemp, in terms of movement and timing, was combined with the stark simplicity of Japanese imagery and the opulence of overbearing Wagnerian opera, Billie Holliday and Mozart. The special effects were stunning and the smoke at times resembled a London peasouper"

- ROUGE

THE PRODUCTION WAS SPONSORED BY
EDWIN SHIRLEY TRUCKING

INTRODUCTION
The Marquis de Sade's 120 Days of Sodom

Sadism is frequently misunderstood as meaning the practice of administering punishment, of causing physical pain as a substitute for "normal" sexual activity; true Sadism however, is far more concerned with the infliction of psychological cruelty, with profound emotional manipulation and distress, with delight in the absolute terror of the Sadist's victim which immediately precedes the execution of violent acts.

Written while Sade was imprisoned in the Bastille, 120 DAYS OF SODOM tells the story of four notorious libertines - a Duke, a Bishop, a Banker and a Judge - who, some time towards the end of the reign of Louis XIV, embark upon a four-month long orgy in a lonely and desolate medieval castle in Switzerland. Four elderly and disease-ridden whores have been recruited as Storytellers whose purpose is to inflame the libertines' jaded passions with nightly tales of staggering perversity.

Sade's motives for the work were twofold. Firstly the academic motive: "Men, already so different from one another in all their other tastes and manias, are even more so sexually; he who could fix and detail all these perversions would accomplish one of the finest moral works one could wish for, and perhaps one of the most interesting ...". The catalogue of perversions recorded within THE 120 DAYS amounts to the first ever *psychopathia sexualis*: it was the better part of a century before the subject was tackled again by *bona fide* scientists.

The second and perhaps more interesting motive behind this work is the ferocious attack upon what Sade perceived to be the corrupt 'Establishment'. The Marquis despised his caste, despised the hypocrisy, amorality and injustice, and was waging his own in-dependent campaign against the Ancien Régime from within, using scandal and outrage as weapons of revolutionary politics; his libertines are usually therefore depicted as pillars of the Establish-ment - aristocrats, clerics and parliamentarians. Sade's aim was nothing less than to strip away every covering, both psychological and physical, from these archetypes and expose them to our disgusted gaze as evil, loathsome monsters. THE 120 DAYS OF SODOM is an anatomy of evil, an epic study of cruelty and excess, counterpointed by a vein of outrageous black humour, and loaded with irony.

Sade was obsessed by the theatre. He acted, directed and wrote many (bad) plays - spurred on, no doubt, by the possibility of manipulating the emotions of his audience. It is of course with the Grand-Guignol, the fin-de-siècle Parisian theatre of blood and horror, that the connection with Sadism becomes most obvious. Audiences came to the Grand-Guignol to be frightened and shocked by the horrifically realistic depiction of murder, mutilation, insanity and sexual violence - and simultaneously to delight in their own terror.

These political and cultural points of reference should be borne in mind to ensure that a stage version of 120 DAYS OF SODOM does not attempt to promote aberration, nor glorify cruelty - even though every theatrical trick and device should be employed to present them as realistically as possible, particularly during the slow, surreal, nightmarish orgy sequences.

Where possible, the Storytellers' tales should be enacted mimetically, according to the whims and/or abilities of the individual actors.

The scene is alternately and simultaneously a prison, a salon, a theatre, an asylum.

NICK HEDGES

photo Stuart Colwill

As the public enters the auditorium, the house lights are already slightly dimmed. Miscellaneous french revolutionary songs play on tape, interspersed with the sound of howling wind.

On stage there are four doors. There is bright light behind them which is seen through cracks in the frames. Soft footlights gently illuminate the doors.

The music is gradually drowned out by the sound of the wind, which begins to howl louder and louder as the house lights and footlights slowly fade to black. The only remaining light is that which escapes from behind the doors. The wind is now louder than ever, then it slowly begins to die down.

Suddenly one of the four doors is flung open: blinding white light and smoke flood through the doorway; at the same time a deafening, interminable, discordant cacophony of sound is heard.

This moment should be held as long as the director dares: just the light, smoke, sound and illuminated doorway. Then, very slowly, Sade appears, backlit, in the doorway - just a silhouette. Very slowly indeed Sade advances to centre stage, whereupon the cacophony abruptly stops. A moment's silence, then the voice of

photo Josephine Wilson/Chris Reid

Sade on tape, with plenty of echo -

SADE   To be alone here ... at the world's end ...
                            Away from all eyes and where no creature
                            can get me ... No barriers, no restraints ...
                            You can't imagine how sensual pleasure is
                            served by such security!

*On tape, a scratching noise begins, like floors being scrubbed and
mixed with this sound, reverberating at different levels and pitches,
are screams, cries, laughs, mutterings, the banging of doors,
wailing.*

*Downstage left is a large wicker crate, the kind for storing theatrical
costumes and paraphernalia.*

*As Sade approaches the crate, the lid slowly lifts by itself, as if by
magic. More bright light and smoke from within. Sade peers inside
and slowly drags out a little girl, semi-nude, clad in dirty linen
underwear, whom he dumps in front of the footlights, facing the
doors. She is motionless.*

Sade turns upstage and extends his arms towards the three closed

photo Stuart Colwill

doors. They slowly open, revealing the Judge, the Duke and the Banker who begin to approach Sade.

Sade returns to the crate and pulls out a large pink powder puff. He powders the wigs and faces of the Judge, the Duke and the Banker - and lastly his own. He then finds his own costume inside the crate and dresses himself as the Bishop. He slowly approaches the Judge and takes hold of the Judge's statute book which will serve as the ledger wherein crimes and punishments will be recorded.

Sade opens the book and turns a few pages. On tape, the amplified, reverberating sound of pages turning. Sade quickly devours the words with his eyes, closes the book, kisses it, and speaks -

SADE: Give a thought to your circumstances! You are beyond the borders of France, high among mountains, in the depths of an uninhabitable forest, and the paths that brought you here were destroyed behind you. No-one on earth knows you are here - you are beyond the reach of your friends and family. In fact, to all intents and purposes, you might as well be dead. And if yet you do breathe, it is by our pleasure and for it only. You must expect naught but humiliation. The only virtue we expect of our guests is obedience - not that you have an awful lot to gain by it, you understand, but because, through disobedience, you have a great deal to lose. Your service will be arduous, it will be painful and rigorous, and the slightest delinquencies will be requited immediately with punishment of the most prodigious severity.

So. The company shall rise every morning at ten. Breakfast will be served at eleven, consisting of chocolate, or roasts cooked in Spanish wine, or other restoratives. Breakfast shall be served by eight young boys, naked, aided by two elders. But it is agreed that at this hour, there shall be no secret or private impudicities.

As it is strictly forbidden for anyone to relieve themselves anywhere save in the Chapel - and forbidden even to go there without special permission, which shall often be refused - all chamberpots shall be scrupulously examined immediately before breakfast, and the names of any offenders will be recorded.

At three shall be served the Masters' lunch, and the honour to serve shall be enjoyed by none but the eight little girls. During the course of the meal, the Masters will be at liberty to handle and touch the unclothed bodies in whatever manner and to whatever extent they please.

Punctually at six o'clock, the appointed Storyteller for that month shall begin her story in the salon, where the entire Company shall convene. Since the object of the narration is to inflame the imagination, every lubricity will be permitted, save for those which might be prejudicial to the approved schedule of deflowerings. Dinner will be served at ten. The meal concluded, the celebrations shall be resumed: everyone shall be sprawled on the floor, and shall, like animals, commingle, entwine, couple incestuously, adulterously, sodomist-ically. And when the deflowerings are due, the operations shall be performed during this period of the day. Once a child be fully initiate, it shall be available thereafter for every enjoyment and at all times.

Such shall be the daily order of procedure. And each Saturday there shall be a common meting out of punishments at the time of the orgies. A detailed register of accumulating delinquencies shall be kept until then.

The least display of mirth, or the least evidence given of disrespect or lack of submission during the debauch activities shall be deemed one of the gravest of faults and shall be one of the most cruelly punished.

Needless to say, should a subject attempt evasion or escape while the assembly is sitting, it shall be punishable instantly by death.

No intrigues among you, no alliances, nor anything remotely resembling an act of religion! I warn you: few crimes will be more severely punished than this one. We know that there are a few in your midst unable to bring themselves to abjure this infamous God and abhor His worship. But decide for yourselves: if there was a God, and if this God had any power at all, would He permit the virtue which honours Him - and which you all profess - to be sacrificed to vice and libertinage as it is going to be?

Those in favour? Those against? Carried.

The little girl in front of the footlights begins to sob quietly. Sade drags her out of the assembly by her hair, beats her, and throws her back into the wicker crate.

The sound of howling wind as slaves set a chaise longue, cushions and a fan. Sade snatches a black sheet off the chaise-longue and the Judge, Banker and Duke take their seats.

Libertines and slaves make themselves comfortable, entwined around each other. During the subsequent tales and debates, everyone is to a greater or lesser degree entwined around one or two other people. A sensual, slowly (but continually) moving chain.

BISHOP: I call upon Madame Duclos!

A slave boy stands and makes a rather fey attempt to blow a fanfare on a trumpet. Madame Duclos, a glamorous but decaying old tart, makes her entrance through one of the back doors. She takes her seat in the middle of the chaise-longue.

DUCLOS: Forgive me, 'tis no slight undertaking, Messieurs, to attempt to express oneself before such a distinguished circle as yours...

JUDGE: We have, I believe, advised you that your narrations must be decorated with the most numerous and searching details -the most minor circumstance, you know, is apt to have an immense influence upon that sensory inflammation we expect from your stories.

DUCLOS: Yes, Your Honour, I have been instructed to omit no detail and to enter into the most minute particulars wherever they may serve to shed light upon the human personality, or upon the species of passion.

DUKE: Excellent. Proceed.

DUCLOS: Well, Messieurs, I was an orphan not yet thirteen when I first learned to flaunt my fanny on the trottoir. Like most unfortunates in my position, I soon found my way to the door of a certain Madame Fournier, who managed a superior establishment not far from the Tuileries Gardens. From then on, there were no more sixpenny shags against alley walls: chez Fournier, I was able to make three crowns from each assignation - although I should perhaps mention that these assignations were frequently of a rather "specialist" nature.

I well recall my first business with a wealthy Arab merchant who took me to the Tuileries not three hours after my arrival at Fournier's. He would have me accost men in the park and frig them six inches from his face while he hid under a pile of folding-chairs. After I had serviced seven or eight passers-by in this manner, he settled himself on a bench by one of the most frequented of the paths, lifted my skirts from behind, and displayed my arse to all and sundry! Then he stuck his doings in the air and bade me frig it well within view of half of Paris, the which, although it was dusk, created such a scandal that by the time he had most cynically unleashed his load, more than ten people had gathered around us, and we were obliged to dash away to avoid being publicly covered with shame.

BISHOP: *(unimpressed)* I've been witness to a dozen such scenes which have cost me a fortune in fuck! There's nothing more pleasant to see or do - for it's just as pleasant to spy upon someone as to want to be observed.

JUDGE: Duclos, I have not the faintest notion of the size of the Arab's article, nor the quantity of discharge. Did he, furthermore, frig your frond the while? You see what I mean about neglected detail ...?

DUCLOS: Forgive me, Your Honour. Despite its brilliant sheen, the Arab's affair was a thing so humble and pitiful that one all but needed spectacles to be certain of its existence. His discharge was rapid, intense and brief, and, I regret to inform you, he did not frig my frond.

JUDGE: There you are - I couldn't visualise a thing at first, but now I can see him clearly!

DUKE: Continue.

DUCLOS: Nigh unto four weeks passed by, during which time no-one of particular interest arrived at Madame Fournier's - that is to say, the gentlemen who called had tastes too ordinary to warrant description - until there came, one afternoon, an old military Captain and veteran of many a campaign on the fields of love. This old roué wanted nothing of we girls, although he did have a particular fondness for the feminine dress ... in short, he wanted to be spanked by a boy got up as a girl; and since he was rich and was willing to pay handsomely for the privilege, we were obliged to drag up the chimney sweep's boy - who was always game, and indeed rather pretty - and whom I armed with a handful of osier switches before introducing to his opponent. And a very interesting contest it was too!

JUDGE: You viewed it?

DUCLOS: Through the keyhole! He began with a careful study of his pretended maiden, and having found him evidently much to his liking, he opened with five or six kisses upon the boy's mouth. Then "Let's be off," cried the Captain! "Ply those switches! Spare not to strike hard!" The lad did everything that was asked of him, happily landing fifty stinging lashes upon a pair of buttocks which only seemed to thirst for more. Already bleeding from those four score stripes and ten, the libertine grabs his masculine flagellatrice, draws up the boy's petticoats, verifies the sex and flings his Adonis back upon the bed, lies down beside him, and simultaneously toys with himself and the boy until both discharge in harmony. I assured the old Captain that I had some charming girlfriends who would be quite happy to flog him and could do so just as well, but he would none of it. He would not so much as look at what my companions and I had to offer.

BISHOP: Oh, I can readily believe that. When one has a taste for men, there's no changing. The difference between a boy and a girl is so extreme that one shouldn't even bother to try what is patently inferior.

DUKE: We could debate that one all night, Monseigneur.

BISHOP: But my dear Blangis, there's nothing to debate: a boy is superior to a girl and that's that.

JUDGE: But for a certain type of pleasure girls are preferable to boys ...

BISHOP: Never! I mean, from the point of view of Evil - Evil almost always being pleasure's true and major charm - the crime must appear greater when perpetrated on a being of your identical sort than when inflicted upon one which is not. This established, the delight automatically doubles.

JUDGE: Yes, but that thrill, that delirium born of the abuse of the weak ...

BISHOP: Well, we all know you're biased because women are more usually subjected to your caprices than males. And besides, women are really no less weak than men: that's just a popular myth. But the point is, provided the man is bound by precisely the same authority that you contrive over women, you will perceive the potential for a greater crime, I assure you, and your lubricity ought to increase twofold.

DUKE: Oh, twofold at least! I agree with the Bishop, Curval: once sovereignty is fully established, the abuse of power has to be more delicious when exercised at the expense of one's peer.

JUDGE: Then we must agree to differ. But gentlemen, I believe these hours have been reserved for listening to the narrations ...?

DUKE: He's right. On with your story, Duclos.

DUCLOS: Thank you, my Lord. Another elderly man, a Clerk at Parliament, with a taste more extraordinary than the last, paid me a call some time afterwards.

Fournier had that day urged me to eat as much as I was able and had served me with everything she knew I liked best - but before we rose from the table, Madame had me swallow down three grains of emetic dissolved in a glass of warm water. The old sinner presently arrived. He was a brothelhound I'd seen around dozens of times before without bothering to find out what he came to do. So. He embraces me ... drives a dirty and disgusting tongue into my mouth ... and the action of the emetic I'd drunk is complemented by his stinking breath. He sees me retch and goes into raptures, lying down on the couch with his head resting on the arm. I unbutton his breeches, drag out a slack and stunted instrument that betrays no sign of stiffening, and which I shake, squeeze, pull ... frigging all the while, as his lascivious hands stray over my buttocks. Suddenly! - at point blank and without warning! - I launch into his mouth the imperfectly digested dinner that the vomitive has fetched up from my stomach ... Our man is beside himself! he rolls his eyes, pants, bolts down the steaming spew, glues his mouth to my lips and by thrusting his foul tongue into my mouth provokes a repetition! And his prick, that worm I've scarcely been able to touch because of my convulsive retchings, weeps delight into my fingers.

And with that, the old bastard coughed, spat, blew his nose, dressed with all possible dispatch - and left.

JUDGE: Now there's a delicious passion indeed, but nevertheless capable of improvement.

DUKE: How so?

JUDGE: Why, by choice of food and partner.

DUKE: Partner? So who would you prefer?

               (casting his eye around the harem)

JUDGE: *(without hesitation)* A stinking, rancid, blind
               beggarwoman. In fact, the more repulsive
               the source, the greater the pleasure! Whoever
               said that youth and beauty are indispensable
               to fuck was a bloody liar!

BISHOP: And the food?

JUDGE: Why, I think I'd force her to give me back,
               in the same manner, all that I'd just given
               her.

DUKE: *(amused, fascinated)* You'd spew into her
               mouth, she'd swallow and then have to blow
               it all back at you?

JUDGE: Precisely.

BISHOP: Heaven!

photo Stuart Colwill

DUKE: Now Duclos, you've come to your fourth and final episode and still you've told us nothing of your childhood or infancy. I can't believe that either was entirely free of lubricity!

JUDGE: Recount your very first adventure!

DUCLOS: Well now Messieurs, as I have already made known, I was a poor orphan brought up by the Nuns. My docility and diligence was rewarded at the end of my sixth year by the special trust of the Mother Superior who charged me with the weekly task of delivering letters of holy business to the Monastery ...

One morning, as I was crossing a little court between the entrance of the Churchyard and the Monastery, I bumped squarely into Father Laurent. He was a monk of about forty with a very handsome face. "Where are you going, little one?" he asked. "Delivering the

Mother's letters," I told him. "I'll take those," said he, "now come along with me - I'm going to show you something you've never seen before ..." And he led me into a sequestered chamber close by, bolting the door behind us. "Now, my little darling," says he, pulling a monstrous engine from his drawers which nearly toppled me with fright, "tell me," he continues, working his fingers back and forth along the length of his horn-hard gristle, "have you ever been curious about the seed wherefrom you were created? Because if you have, my poppet, I've quite a treat in store for you ... lend a hand now ... help it along... If you do this for me, then I shall give you a precious gift ... a special something ... to adorn that swanlike neck of yours ... and that plump ... young ... breast ..." With that, his face turns scarlet and four or five gobs of shiny white glue land on my pinafore. Seeing my bewilderment, Father Laurent smiles. "There my dear," says he, "and how do you like your new pearl necklace? My, how it suits you ... how pretty you look!"

Gradually regaining control of himself, he calmly put his tool away, slipped sixpence into my hand and suggested I might bring to him any little friends I happened to have. Now I loved the Nuns and I worshipped Virtue, but I grew to love money more ... and in the space of three months I supplied Father Laurent with more than twenty little orphans.

DUKE: Thank you Madame Duclos!

Applause from the company, cries of bravo, and Madame Duclos rises and exits through the door whence she came.

DUKE: Monsieur Curval, I do suspect your prick is in the air ...!

BISHOP: Will you be purged of a little something, Curval?

JUDGE: Not everyone's like you, you know, flinging
                    his fuck this way and that every five minutes!
                    I leave that kind of vulgar display to virtuosi
                    like yourself!

*A girl from the harem rises and slowly approaches the Bishop. She
raises her skirts, hoping to satisfy his evident needs.*

GIRL: *(mock-erotic)* Bless me Father, for I have
                    sinned ...

BISHOP: Oh, for God's sake put that cunt away! I
                    certainly don't want any of that! These
                    thick little whores ... never have anything
                    but cunt to show you ... Now I probably
                    won't be able to discharge for the rest of the
                    evening unless I can get the image of that
                    accursed cunt out of my head! Give me an
                    arse someone!

*The Banker lowers his breeches and offers his own arse to the
Bishop (who regards it through a telescope). Meanwhile the girl
has moved along to the Judge and the lascivious commingling
resumes.*

photo Josephine Wilson/Chris Reid

BANKER: In order to enhance the lubricious properties of discharge by alerting the assembled company to the moment of its occurrence, that they may share in it howso'er they choose, I propose that the dinner gong be struck upon each and every attainment of crisis by any member of the company whomso'er he be, Master or Slave. For? Against? Carried!

A boy begins to sob quietly. The Banker drags him out of the assembly by his hair, beats him and throws him back into the wicker crate. As the lid is slammed shut, the Judge strikes the gong and lights a cigarette. On tape, 'Dance of the Seven Veils' from 'Salome' by Strauss.

Red and yellow lights come up slowly. The company is costumed in Turkish/Arabian fancy dress. Incense burns. A Moorish dance to appropriate music. When it ends, they applaud each other and sink back into the cushions, resuming their lascivious couplings. An hermaphrodite brings sweetmeats and fruits on a silver platter, which the Masters eat out of their partners' mouths, in between kisses.

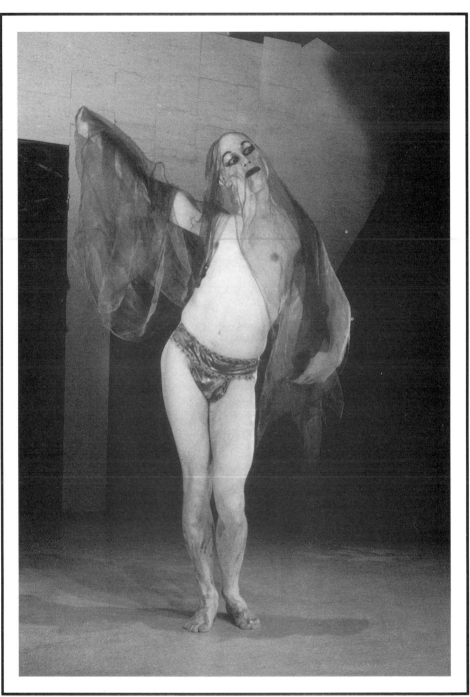

photo Josephine Wilson/Chris Reid

The gong is struck again. A large 'parcel' is lifted out of the crate: it is wrapped in sheets and strips of fabric. Each time the Strauss stops, a layer of cloth is removed from the parcel. The game continues until the 'prize' is won by the Bishop: a pretty boy in very cheap drag. They kiss as the others continue to kiss, eat and commingle.

The dragged-up boy begins to dance, discarding his 'seven veils' as he does so. He is encouraged by the others with whom he flirts and exchanges kisses while he dances. The atmosphere is one of warmth and sensuality, of mutual pleasure.

The soft footlights are replaced by a stark white spotlight, and the dancing boy, now almost naked, is seized by the libertines. He struggles, is beaten and then held aloft. With only a single spotlight on him, the boy appears suspended about six or seven feet in the air. From below, disembodied hands beat him with nettles and holly. Now the Bishop too is held aloft behind the boy. The boy's legs are held apart and he is deflowered by the Bishop. Both are lowered to the ground and all the men take it in turn to bugger the boy. The Duke is handed a rubber glove and a knuckleduster. Wearing both, he proceeds to fistfuck the boy.

photo Stuart Colwill

The noise of howling wind which fades as the lights come up slowly: a blue wash, moonlight. Relaxation. Only two or three actors remain, sprawled on the cushions, semi-naked. All take a puff from the hookah, and movement slows to absolute stillness. As a distant clock chimes eight, white light is gradually added to the blue. Two girls and a boy enter in nightgowns, with their hands behind their backs. The Bishop and the Banker rise, the Banker holding the punishment book. The girls and boy bring out their chamber pots from behind their backs which they hold out for inspection.

The first girl's is empty ... the boy's is empty ... the second girl's is full. The Bishop and Banker confer and the Banker enters the delinquent's name in the punishment book, while the Bishop ties a black ribbon around her wrist. The children are about to leave when the Bishop calls back the second girl. On tape, musique concrète, as the Banker produces a silver spoon which he hands to the Bishop, who in turn hands it to the girl. Despite her tears, her pleading and her retching, she is forced to eat her own shit with a silver spoon, while the Bishop and Banker look on, fascinated. On tape, the scrubbing and wailing sounds are added to the musique concrète. The girl's face is pushed into the chamberpot as the libertines take it in turn to sniff and lick the spoon.

photo Stuart Colwill

Eventually the Bishop strikes the gong to denote orgasm, then The Banker strikes it repeatedly to announce breakfast.

The lights come full up as the rest of the company enter the salon, followed by an hermaphrodite, who holds a silver meat dish. He lifts the lid to reveal a Kellogg's mini variety pack of breakfast cereals which he distributes to the assembled company. They eat the cereal dry with their hands.

BANKER: Madame Champville!

Madame Champville enters through a different door to her predecessor. Again, she takes pride of place on the chaise-longue. She too is well past her sell-by date, perhaps looking like Elizabeth Taylor at the height of her drink and drugs problem. Applause as she enters.

BANKER: Now Champville, if you are as equal to your assignment as Madame Duclos, then you too will be rewarded with gentle treatment - whatever choice horrors might befall the others - as well as a safe return to Paris. Do I make myself clear?

photo Stuart Colwill

CHAMPVILLE: Quite clear, sir.

BISHOP: Then you may proceed, Madame.

CHAMPVILLE: I know not, Messieurs, whether you have ever heard tell of the infamous tastes exercised by a certain Parisian Magistrate of my acquaint ... This gentleman had a little apartment looking out upon the Place de Grève where executions were often held. Whenever preparations began for such an event, the Magistrate would immediately send a cab for me and we would repair to his salon, the casement window of which commanded a direct view of the scaffold. We would post ourselves there, he and I, behind a lattice-work screen upon one of whose horizontal slats he rested a really rather excellent pair of opera glasses.

Finally the crowd's hubbub would announce the victim's arrival, and the Magistrate would have me frig him, gently, proportioning my strokes to the progress of the execution ... the criminal stepped up upon the platform, the jurist contemplated him; the victim knelt, the more furious became the jurist's prick in my hands; the axe was raised ... the axe was brought down - and at that instant my friend discharged, just as the villain rendered up his soul to God! "Ah, gentle Jesus," he'd say, "double-fucked Christ! How I'd love to be the executioner myself, and how much better I'd swing the blade!" "But your Honour," I said to him on one occasion, "through your public office you have co-operated in the destruction of this poor victim". "That's precisely what gives me the thrill," said he, "I've been on the bench for thirty years and have never pronounced any but the death sentence!"

JUDGE: I dare say only a pregnant woman for a victim would have a stronger effect on me.

BISHOP: Oh, well of course one must learn how to

refine the horror ... but in horror there is undoubtedly matter for producing an erection, and the moment that even the most frightful imagining acquires the power to make you discharge, 'tis no longer horrible - save in the eyes of others. But then, who is to assure me that the opinion of others, which is almost always faulty or erroneous in every other case, is not equally so in this instance?

JUDGE: Nothing's villainous if it causes an erection - in fact, the one villainy that exists in the world is to deny oneself anything that might produce one!

BANKER: There is nothing fundamentally evil.

JUDGE: Nor anything fundamentally good - everything is relative.

BISHOP: To our point of view!

BANKER: Vite, Madame, continuez!

CHAMPVILLE: The man with whom I held correspondence directly after the one whose example has just seduced you, insisted that the woman with whom he was presented had indigestion. To this end, his housekeeper, who had given me no foreknowledge of the thing, had me during dinner swallow a laxative drug which softened what my bowels contained, indeed rendered it fluid. Our man arrives and I bid him start without delay since I was by now painfully inflated with gases. Whereupon he raises my skirts, parts my cheeks, and glues his mouth hermetically to my arsehole as his tongue strives to penetrate the chasm. That does it! The floodgates open and he swallows everything, asking for still more. Well, what can you do ....? I furnish him with a second deluge, which is swiftly followed by a third!

BANKER: Excellent! Now there's a man I'm hugely fond of already!

JUDGE: You know, for taste of shit, there's nothing to equal what one gets from a child who has just heard the death sentence pronounced against its mother.

The Banker shrieks with laughter. The Bishop strikes the gong.

BISHOP: I suggest, gentlemen, that nothing is more logical than to adore degradation: he who ardently loves the things which dishonour and degrade must necessarily derive pleasure from submitting to such practices himself. There's no saying how far you could go, provided you're ashamed of nothing ... I've heard of certain ill persons whom nothing delights like the disintegration of their own diseased bodies.

JUDGE: And all this is to say nothing of the pleasure to be derived from the punishment and public disgrace. We all know the story of the brave Marquis de Sade who, when informed of the Magistrates' decision to burn him in effigy, pulled his prick from his breeches and said, "God be fucked, it's taken them years to do it, but it's done at last! Dripping in infamy, am I? Then leave me, leave me, for I've absolutely got to discharge!" And so he did, in less time than it takes to tell!

BANKER: I don't dispute it, but why should it be so?

BISHOP: Once a man has debased himself through excess, he has imparted something of a vicious cast upon his soul which nothing can repair. In any other case shame would act as a deterrent, but here that possibility has been eliminated altogether. All that used to affect one so disagreeably is now transformed into sheer pleasure potential.

BANKER: I propose that the cooks be ordered to modify our guests' diet: all breads, heavy soups and vegetables shall be forbidden, and replaced by chicken breast, boned fowl and prunes, which shall be consumed in immense quantities only for breakfast, lunch, high tea and dinner. This new menu should, I hope, produce two bowel movements per day of an exceeding soft and sweet variety.

The Judge strikes the gong.

BANKER: Those in favour? Against? Carried! Madame ...?

CHAMPVILLE: A Police Chief - a notorious bugger - kidnapped a father and daughter on the highway and imprisoned them in a dark dungeon. There, with a pistol held to the man's head, he forced the father to fuck his own daughter, after which he roped the two victims together and sodomised both. Next, he informs the father that the girl must die,

photo Stuart Colwill

but offers him the choice of killing her himself, by strangling, which will be quick and cause little pain; or, if he prefers not to kill his own child, then he, the Police Chief will do the work, but the father shall have to witness it all, and the girl's agonies will be atrocious. Rather than see her undergo frightful tortures, the father decides to kill his daughter with a noose of black silk, but while he is preparing to dispatch her, he is seized, bound, and before his eyes his child is flayed alive and thrown into a bonfire. The father is strangled. This, says the libertine, is to teach him a lesson not to be so eager to choke the life out of his own children, for 'tis barbaric.

BANKER: Hear, hear!

JUDGE: *(heated)* By fuck, the whore's story has got me stiff! I could easily be persuaded to go abroad right now and rob a carriage!

- 35 -

BISHOP: So long as its occupants were poor - else where would be the pleasure in't?

JUDGE: That goes without saying, of course.

BISHOP: God's arse, I despise charity! Those absurd and revolting relief enterprises ... they outrage Nature by upsetting the order she imposed when she created different classes of individuals!

BANKER: There must be rich in order that there can be poor, any fool knows that! Wealth guarantees the spectacle of poverty.

BISHOP: And what a spectacle! What a passion is inflamed by the persecution of the sick and needy!

JUDGE: What, Bishop?? You mean, you would not give succour to the lowly and wretched ...??

BISHOP: Like hell, I would! Were I to help the beggars taste but an instant's happiness, it would completely destroy the distinction between them and myself, thus destroying all the pleasure afforded by the comparison.

JUDGE: Sometimes I think it would be better simply to hang the poor and be done with it.

BANKER: For sure crime has sufficient charm of its own without having to resort to any secondary activity. I myself owe pints of fuck to stealing, murder, arson and such like. It's not the idea of libertine intention which fires me - just the pure ecstasy of evil.

BISHOP: And thence is born another certitude: the more pleasure you seek in the depths of crime, the more frightful the crime must be.

BANKER: Do you have anything to add, Madame Champville?

CHAMPVILLE: Only that this same villain of whom I spoke, in order to combine incest, adultery, sodomy and blasphemy ...

BANKER:
BISHOP: } Buggered his own married daughter with a crucifix!
JUDGE:

BANKER: Many thanks, Madame Champville, many thanks indeed!

In the darkness, Monteverdi's "Ego Flos Campi" plays on tape. The pattern and colours of a stained glass window fade up, projected onto a large piece of white cloth which slowly falls to the ground as a shaft of white light illuminates the scene. We discover that the white cloth was the train of a wedding dress held aloft. The Bishop is standing with his back towards us, marrying a young boy and girl, who face us. The Bishop slowly exits as the young couple kiss and petals fall on them from above.

The Monteverdi ends, and the Bacchanale from Wagner's "Tannhauser" begins as the company enter, playing wedding guests, dressed in mythological costume (Venus, Adonis, Cupid, Diana, etc). The white cloth, the train of the girl's dress, is detached and pulled taut along a diagonal, suggesting a table. The guests, all of whom are behind it, raise glasses and toast the couple, who are in front of the cloth, dancing together, slowly and sensually.

The cloth is snatched away and slowly lain over the chaise-longue and the guests light candles around it before departing. The lights fade, leaving the couple to finish their dance in a spotlight which eventually fades as a soft light on the chaise-longue is slowly illuminated. Silence. Slowly, hesitantly, the couple make their way over to the chaise-longue, where they kiss and tentatively begin to undress each other, but suddenly become aware of the Bishop and the Judge who have just stepped into the circle of light and are eyeing the couple lasciviously. The libertines make slow, stylised gestures of encouragement, but to no avail: the dreamy sensual atmosphere has been broken. What follows between the couple is crude, embarrassed, clumsy, and they are unable to complete the wedding ritual by consummating their marriage.

photo Josephine Wilson/Chris Reid

The Bishop and the Judge are furious and the punishment book and black ribbons are produced ... but the libertines have had their attention drawn by a noise in the shadows. Torches are lit, and a couple are discovered having an illicit encounter in the darkness. The libertines are more furious than ever. The delinquents' names are entered in the ledger and black ribbons are tied around their wrists. They are branded with smoking irons, then forced to assist the libertines who are anxious to deflower the young married couple. The beribboned delinquents hold down first the girl and then the boy, while the libertines violently rape them (lots of blood), as the Wagner climaxes. Blackout.

Spotlight up on the Bishop, licking his fingers.

BISHOP: Madame Martaine!

Madame Martaine is illuminated sitting astride a chair (à la Marlene). Accompanied on an accordion, she sings a splendidly sleazy rendition of "My Blue Heaven" (Whiting/Donaldson).

> *"When the whippoorwills call*
> *And the evening is nigh*

photo Stuart Colwill

I hurry to my

Blue heaven

I turn to the right

A little white light

Will lead you to my

Blue heaven

You see a smiling face

A fireplace

A cosy room

A little nest, that's nestled where

The roses bloom

Just my honey and me

And baby makes three

We're happy in my

Blue heaven"

(REPEAT)

Applause as the lights come up. Exit Madame Martaine.

DUKE: If happiness consists in the absolute
satisfaction of all the senses, then I swear it

would be difficult to be more happy than we!

BISHOP: What kind of remark is that? It is not a libertine's! How on earth can you be happy if you are constantly able to satisfy yourself? It is not desire's consummation in which happiness exists, but in the desire itself, in overcoming the barriers set in front of one's desires. I mean, here one only needs wish and one has - where's the satisfaction in that? I swear to you that since the party began, my fuck has not once flowed because of the objects I find about me: every time I have discharged upon contemplation of what is not here.

JUDGE: My dear Blangis, I think the one essential thing lacking to our happiness is the sight of true misery ... the sight of he who does not in the least enjoy what we enjoy - and who suffers! Thence comes the pleasure of being able to say, "I am happier than he!"

DUKE: You know Durcet, I do believe you're right...

BISHOP: I know what you're thinking gentlemen ... the punishment book! Those in favour? Against? Carried!

The Judge hands the punishment book to the Bishop, who in turns hands it to the Duke. The Duke glances through it to reacquaint himself with some of the misdemeanours, while the Bishop and the Judge drag two victims out of the assembly.

The two victims, a boy and a girl, are roped together. The Duke slices a strip of flesh from the girl's shoulder which he hands to the Judge, who eats it. The Duke kisses the girl's wound and she faints. Meanwhile the Bishop gouges out one of the boy's eyes. Both victims collapse and the libertines notice the little girl with a black ribbon tied around her wrist: she is scratching at the doors with bleeding fingers.

The Bishop slowly unties the girl's black ribbon and uses it to blindfold her. Then he begins to slowly spin the girl around to disorientate her, and all the light fades to black, save that from a

photo Stuart Colwill

bare bulb hanging above. The Bishop knocks the bulb so that it swings, then he releases his grip upon the girl and retires into the shadows.

On tape, the sound of smashing glass. The terrified girl careers around, in and out of the swinging spotlight's beam, trying to avoid the glass. The girl becomes more and more terrified and increasingly exhausted too. Finally she falls to the floor and breaks down.

The sound of the breaking glass stops and the swinging bulb comes to a standstill. The Bishop steps into the light and sits the girl on a chair. He unties her blindfold, she is sobbing hysterically and pleads for leniency. The Bishop begins to kiss her ... though still crying, the girl makes an effort to respond, hoping to buy a little respite with sexual favours. She closes her eyes and opens her mouth to kiss the Bishop, who produces a pistol and puts the barrel of it into her mouth. The girl opens her eyes and is shaking with terror, The Bishop is fascinated and amused by her fear. He withdraws the gun from the girl's mouth, turns his back on her and walks away. Just as she begins to relax, the Bishop turns and shoots her dead.

photo Stuart Colwill

The footlights come full up, casting shadows as they illuminate the entire company dressed in black (veils, etc.) and holding candles. On tape, "Liebestod" from Wagner's "Tristan and Isolde". The girl's corpse is ceremonially wrapped in a black sheet and lowered into the wicker crate. As the lid is slammed shut, the music cuts and the lights come full up.

JUDGE: And finally, pray silence for Madame Desgranges!

The final door opens. In contrast to her three predecessors, Madame Desgranges is a stunningly beautiful young woman, impeccably and expensively dressed and bejewelled, with great dignity and charisma. She takes her place on the chaise-longue. The lascivious coupling resumes around her.

DESGRANGES: Gentlemen ... an infamous libertine whose mistress I was had a particular passion to see a little girl mounted by a dog. At the very moment the dog discharged, my master shot it dead, leaving the little girl terrified, but relatively unharmed. He would then have her introduce a serpent into her younger

- 45 -

brother's rectum. As the little boy was thus embuggered he screamed in agony - and all the while I was enjoined to flog my master senseless.

BANKER: *(leaping to his feet and scanning the assembled company)* O Sacred Satan, I will pay the Society two hundred pounds right now for leave to fuck a maiden arse!

JUDGE: Steady Durcet, you know we must not depart from the approved schedule. Please Madame...

DESGRANGES: This libertine, my master, had spies keep regular watch near the cemeteries to bring word every time there was a burial of some young child. As soon as he got news of something suitable, we would set off after sundown, enter the cemetery by one means or another, heading at once for the grave our spy had indicated. Finding the earth only recently broken, we would both fall to work until we had dug up the corpse, Once we'd uncovered it, I'd frig my master over it while he spent his time handling its buttocks. If perchance - and it frequently happened - he stiffened a second time, he'd therewith shit, and have me shit also, upon the corpse, and finally discharge thereupon, all the while fingering whatever parts of the body he could lay his hands on.

DUKE: But would he not say anything during the ritual?

DESGRANGES: Oh, he would naturally shower invectives upon the deceased - "Swim in my fuck to hell, you cunt", that sort of thing.

DUKE: Hmm, not an entirely unknown taste ...

BISHOP: I bet he didn't stop there though! I bet - Blangis! You're fucking your daughter!

BANKER: I swear he imagined her dead!

DUKE:	Well, of course! How else in the world could I have discharged? Continue, Desgranges!
DESGRANGES:	On another occasion, I was witness to a delightful operation my master performed upon our serving maid, Lucille, who had been engaged less for her domestic diligence than for her proven virginity which had been confirmed by a prior medical examination.
	She is shown into the boudoir for her first audience of the Master: "Well? What the devil are you doing standing there?" says he, in a harsh voice. "Do I have to tell you to get your skirts up? I should have been looking at your arse two hours ago!" "But Monsieur," said Lucille, "what am I to do?" "What are you to do? Why pick up your skirts and show me that damned arse I'm paying to see!" Lucille obeys, trembling like a leaf, and reveals a little white bum just

as darling and sweet as that of Venus herself. "Oh, I suppose it'll do ..." murmurs my man. "Now, do you want to shit?" he asks. "No, Monsieur". "Well, I do. In fact, I've got something quite hefty to get rid of, so lie down on the couch and get your legs open!" Lucille settles herself and the Master poses her so that her wide-flung thighs display her cunt to the fullest advantage -in which open position it may be readily employed as a chamberpot: for so to use it was his singular intention.

He takes his place ... pushes ... and lands a turd in that sanctuary Cupid himself would not have disdained having for a temple. He turns around, eyes his work, and with his fingers, presses and thrusts the filthy excrement into the rose-lipped ouverture and largely out of sight. Lucille utters a cry, and by means of this charming operation loses the precious flower, Nature's ornament, given the child as a gift to Hymen.

This was the moment at which our libertine's pleasure attained its crisis: to have filled the young and pretty hole with shit, to crowd it to overflowing and to stuff it yet more, this was his supreme delight. Having concluded his business, I was charged with utmost care to clean the soiled area with my tongue.

BANKER: Well, by God, there's a bit of taxing drudgery I own! But then, I ask you, what the devil is a woman's tongue good for if not to wipe arseholes? I frankly cannot think of any other use to put it to.

BISHOP: Why, once again 'tis the filthy act that causes the greatest pleasure - and the filthier it be, the more copiously fuck is shed!

DUKE: Look what I've got here! Look at this little whore's arse, Curval! What shall I do with it?

JUDGE: Douse it in vinegar sauce!

DUKE: What an excellent jest!

The gong is struck and the Duke and the Banker rise in anticipation of the orgy.

JUDGE: But first do Madame Desgranges the honour
                    of allowing her to complete her narration.

BANKER: *(incredulous)* Can there still be more?

DESGRANGES: You may readily imagine my surprise,
                    gentlemen, the night my pagan Master led
                    me to a deserted Chapel ... Seating me upon
                    the altar, he proceeded to frig me with a
                    golden crucifix, which then he drove hard
                    into my cunt and fucked me, discharging
                    upon it in his turn. He then bade me frig him
                    until he discharged upon the Host, and when
                    he was restored to perfect calm after his fuck
                    had flowed, he fed wafer and all to a wild
                    dog. Then he pisses and bade me piss into

the chalice also; he shits thereinto and has me shit thereinto, whereupon he promptly discharges therein. Finally he breaks up a large crucifix, smashes several images of the Virgin and the Eternal Father, shits upon the debris and burns the whole fucking mess.

The following day, we returned to the scene of the crime for Evensong and frigged each other while listening to the word of God.

BISHOP: *(blasé)* You know, it seems to me that one never sufficiently exploits the possible ... I'm convinced one can go still further than that.

BANKER: Further than that?? And what the devil would you have us do?

BISHOP: Worse! - Even were it to dismember Nature and unhinge the universe!

photo Josephine Wilson/Chris Reid

The gong is struck repeatedly. Blackout. On tape, "Descent into Hell" from Mozart's "Don Giovanni". A flash of lightning and a flood of smoke, lit with red light.

A door is flung open, revealing a backlit religious statue. In a decadent parody of the end of "Don Giovanni", the libertines invite the statue to dine with them - feeding it shit from their chamberpots. The stage is flooded with smoke and the statue is seized, undressed and gangbanged before the libertines shit over its face. Blackout.

The Mozart cuts to a few bars of Nat King Cole's recording of "The Party's Over" (Styne/Green/Comden). A moment of stillness as a tattered French flag is held aloft. Then, heavily amplified, the sound of the guillotine's blade falling. The flag falls to the floor, revealing behind it the Bishop, spotlit in darkness. On tape, the scrubbing/ wailing noise begins again. Shadowy "doctors" remove the Bishop's hat, mask and costume, revealing Sade. The "doctors" then remove Sade's wig and jacket, revealing him to be in a straitjacket.

The footlights come up slowly, softly illuminating other asylum inmates who are scrubbing the floor with the scrunched up flag.

One "doctor" opens the same door through which Sade entered. White light and smoke flood through the doorway. As Sade is very slowly escorted towards the door, the cacophony fades up on tape, reaching its loudest point as all the lights - except those behind the door - go out.

As Sade steps through the door, the sound cuts and blackout.

A few seconds' silence and then on tape, a recording of Billie Holiday singing "For Heaven's Sake Let's Fall in Love" (Meyer/ Bretton/Edwards). At the end of the first verse, the footlights come up slowly, illuminating the whole company and a series of slow curtain calls are taken. Blackout.

THE END

AN INTERVIEW WITH NICK HEDGES

Q: **So, Nick, how the hell could you conceive of making THE 120 DAYS into a play?**

NH: Paul Blackman, the Producer, liked the title, thought it had a charming ring to it! I was initially interested in some kind of hybrid of **Justine** and **Juliette**, the books that have been getting Arrow a hard time. But **120 Days** is much stronger. It encapsulates all the extremes, all the pleasures, all the vices.

Q: **How has the relationship been with the Producer?**

NH: We're just good friends! Paul is enthusiastic about my work and wanted to give it free reign, wanted to find the right sort of material to create exciting possibilities, that is. He suggested the Marquis de Sade and I reeled off the titles. **The 120 Days of Sodom** - what a catchy title! He's been very supportive all the way through, particularly when there have been legal problems, or problems with the local council. He's seen the thing in context and is prepared to argue the validity of presenting the philosophy. He's brave, imaginative, committed - everything you could possibly want in a Producer.

Q: It's a heavily stylised play, isn't it?

NH: Yes, it has to be. I mean, you can't just do all the atrocities on stage. That's not particularly theatrical: it's Snuff Theatre. We have to make the ugliness beautiful somehow. We're faithful to the spirit of Sade, but it's not naturalistic. There's none of what I call "bedroom acting" - big performances which you should only do in front of your bedroom mirror. The final punishments - gouged eyes and torn flesh - are presented in the style of French Grand-Guignol Theatre, which, in the 1880's and 90's, was the forerunner of today's 'splatter' movies. It seemed a legitimate source to draw on for a show like this. We're also making use of opera - particularly **Don Giovanni**, Mozart's opera about an infamous libertine which was written at the same time as **120 Days**. Added to that is a bit of Japanese theatre - the rituals of Noh and the sufferings of Butoh seemed especially apt - it slows everything down almost to a still life, which is a great way of depicting the punishment scenes. There's also a strong element of black comedy, of course, a touch of camp. There's a torch song, a bit of jazz - one of the old whores sings **My Blue Heaven**. It's all deliberately chaotic, anachronistic, a brightly-coloured collage of impressions and ideas.

Q: **How about other influences? Would Artaud be relevant?**

NH: Yes, of course - but not too specifically. I'm more influenced by paintings and music. And sculpture. Museums. Artefacts. (laughs) That's what I'm really doing, sculpting with flesh. And of course opera is a big influence - Wagner, Mozart.

Q: **Are you particularly influenced by any authors, not necessarily playwrights?**

NH: Cocteau, of course, Nabokov, Crowley ... Aleister Crowley. I did a production of **The Tempest** which based Prospero on him. His and Crowley's were the same story - Prospero was a magician, kicked off the mainland for becoming "transported, rapt in secret studies". He had to continue his magic in isolation, on an island. Same story as Crowley. So we used a lot of Crowley's rituals and made Prospero look like one of those fabulous self-portraits Crowley painted.

And the harpy in **"The Tempest"** was Crowley's "Scarlet Woman". So we found quite a few parallels to play around with. I wasn't for one moment suggesting it was a precise parallel, but there was definitely theatrical mileage in it. I'm so attracted to those unique, extraordinary big personalities. People who live without fear of ostracism.

Q: In some ways they can afford to.

NH: XH!H!G Crowley couldn't! But he persuaded people to support his experiments - his acolytes bankrupted themselves to keep him in heroin! I love con artists and charlatans. I'm attracted to Andy Warhol too. I mean, I don't subscribe to the idea that he was a conman, but there was some big operating going on there, definitely. I'm fascinated by that whole "Factory" scene ... and his work is so simple, so beautiful. I'm planning a dance-theatre project based on Warhol's life and art.

Q: Is gothic literature an influence?

NH: Not directly. Victorian literature, yes, and fairy tales. I don't really enjoy much after 1920, except, as I said, Cocteau and Nabokov - and John Berryman's poetry. He was a manic depressive and all his poems are steeped in madness and despair, illuminated occasionally by flashes of the most delicious black comedy and unexpectedly tender affirmations of love. John Berryman is wonderful - not to be confused with John Betjeman!

Q: Do you feel you have anything in common with Peter Greenaway or Derek Jarman?

NH: I'm certainly not influenced by either of them. I quite like one or two of their films, they share a painterly quality which is occasionally quite stunning. Greenaway is sometimes witty, but ultimately too sterile, clinical, unengaging. Jarman's fantasies are enchanting, but for me his big mistake is his insistence on working in modern allegories and issues which is always so clumsy. I think that those two are obviously quite important directors, but I confess I feel more aligned, spiritually and artistically, with Ken Russell and John Waters. Lindsay is the biggest influence though, Lindsay Kemp. He's a dancer, a painter, a magician ... a genius! He opened my eyes to so much. You go to his classes and you fall in love. If you share that same world-view, you fall in love with him and you want to help, do what you can, be that performing or assisting in some other way. You do anything for him. No-one in the world knows more about making **electric** theatre than Lindsay - and his life and performances are all wrapped up in themselves, inseparable, that's why being around him is so exhilarating and inspiring. He's on stage the whole time. He dances through life. Like his ancestor, Will Kempe, who left Shakespeare's company and danced from London to Norwich.

Q: How do you feel you fit into British Theatre, if indeed you do?

NH: I don't know. I don't really analyse what I do - it's all instinct. It comes from the heart, not the head. But I certainly don't think I'm anything to do with that awful, dry literary theatre with its stultifying academic tradition. Theatre ought to engage the senses, not pander to the intellect. The kind of thing I do asks to be **felt**, not understood. I think perhaps the British are suspicious of that way of working, whereas it's readily embraced on the Continent. And of course the British like to categorise, but what I do isn't really theatre, isn't really dance - it's a collage of pantomime and cabaret and Japanese theatre ... and a whole lot more besides. It's indefinable. And I'm drawn repeatedly to the same kind of subject matter - the process whereby the solitary artist, possessed by a forbidden desire, creates an imaginary world in which that desire can be realised. You can see it in **The Tempest, 120 Days, Lolita ...** But then if you write, you don't want to be a journalist, do you? You want to be a poet. And the best poets are those who return again and again to the same subjects. They asked me on the radio about **The Tempest** - why did I choose to do it? I said, well dear, I couldn't decide which Pinter to do. He wrote so many wonderful plays. There's **The Homecoming, The Caretaker ...** I just couldn't make up my mind ... So I thought, what the hell, do a Crowley Shakespeare! (laughs)

Q: You obviously enjoy playing up to interviewers.

NH: Crafty denials and crafty non-denials - I kind of share that with Sade, I think. I'm quite prepared to tell anyone anything they want hear, really. And if someone urges me to flirt a bit more, then I'm obliged to go that little bit further. This woman at the BBC was winding me up about **120 Days**, she was saying (adopts Americanised "meejah" voice) "Come on, are they nude? What are they doing? Do they do this? Do they do that?" I said, well there's some fistf- She said, "Yes, I think we've got the picture!" She finished up by asking if I thought the show would run its whole length - which was a gift of a feed line. I said, Darling you know what they say, length isn't important ...

Q: Did Peter Weiss' Marat/Sade influence you at all?

NH: No, not at all. I'm not very familiar with that play. I gather there are similarities, but I think that play was just a vehicle for exploring Peter Brook's version of Artaud - which is unforgivable. You should find the subject matter first and then suit your method to it, not the other way round.

Q: How relevant a figure do you think Sade is to a modern audience?

NH: Do you know that series the Sunday Times has been running on Makers of the Twentieth Century ...? If you were to create a series on Makers of History, you'd have to include Sade. As a philosopher, part-time politician and agent provocateur during the build up to the French Revolution. His prison term, and the loneliness that arose from it, which caused him to channel his libido - indeed, **all** his passions - into his writing. There was a peculiar clash of politics, sex and philosophy. Scientists, philosophers, sexologists and politicians have all dealt with their respective areas more profoundly, but Sade was writing at least a hundred years before most of them.

Q: What is Sade's relevance to you, personally?

NH: What is his relevance to me, **personally?** (laughs) Well, I like a challenge ...! I like the bad taste - keeping the tongue in the cheek despite the horrors. When you watch **Salo*** you realise that Pasolini was probably what we've come to understand by the term 'sadist'. Because I don't think there's any humour in it.

*   **Pier Paolo Pasolini's cinematic updating of 120 days to fascist Italy.**

Q: **There's no humour, but it's also more allegorical, in that the libertines are shown to be fascists.**

NH: Sure, but it's also to do with modern sadists, as I understand it, liking their role-playing done with utmost seriousness. As the Bishop says at the beginning of the play, "the least display of mirth shall be deemed one of the gravest of faults". Whereas when Sade wrote it, there was certainly a degree mirth there.

Q: **Of course - they're meant to be having fun, aren't they?**

NH: Ye-eah, but I think he was having fun as well. There's a lot of black comedy.

Q: **So you think a lot of Sade's critics are misguided?**

NH: They're very misguided - they take it all too literally. As they've all being doing with **Juliette**, taking four lines out of context. Those four lines - yes, they're horrific, but you have to see the thing as a whole to understand Sade's real intentions. He was using outrage as a weapon of revolutionary politics.

Q: **What about Andrea Dworkin? Have you read her criticism of Sade?**

NH: No, I haven't. What does she say?

Q: **Her basic criticism is that Justine and Juliette are both men's fantasies, even though Sade states that they are about a strong woman and a weak woman respectively. Dworkin says that Sade is merely fulfilling and reinforcing male fantasies about two female stereotypes.**

NH: No, I don't think that Sade can be read as that kind of fantasy because there's no tease it in, no slow, lingering build up to the acts. There has to be an element of tease for things to work as erotica or pornography. That's absent in Sade's work, and deliberately so. It's a discussion of evil.

Q: **Are the wicked libertines in 120 Days Sade's prison cell projections of himself, given absolute freedom?**

NH: There are no real characters in the play. They're just symbols - the Duke, the Bishop, the Banker, the Judge. Their actions are so excessive, it's almost a kind of camp.

That's how we're playing it - lull the audience into a false sense of security - "Oh, this is really quite a giggle" - then throw in all the other elements, from torch song through to abject horror. The libertines also double as the whores. The ritual of dragging-up is true to Sade.

Q: **You say you see them as symbols. Is that symbols of the corruption of people in positions of power?**

NH: Yes, but above all they're archetypes. Sade conceived them as archetypes, and we've portrayed them not as real characters, but as almost pantomime archetypes. The important thing is to avoid all notions of character motivation!

Q: **In the original book they're obviously archetypes as well. But what do they represent?**

NH: They represent the pillars of the establishment - the Church, the Law, Money, the Aristocracy.

Q: **The way I read the book and the play is that these people are symbols of the corruption of their times.**

NH: It's a moral tale ... (laughs)

Q: **Of course it is. That's what we've been telling everyone.**

NH: It's an horrifically exaggerated political cartoon.

Q: **In a way, that's what Salo was showing - Salo was an anti-fascist film.**

NH: Yeah, but something about that film worries me. I feel he maybe used the allegory to conceal his own tastes.

Q: **Quite possibly, but he's not alive to refute it. Anyway, how did you recruit your actors. Were any of them put off by the content?**

NH: Well the material is rather unpleasant and difficult to come to terms with ... Stylistically, I think it was a challenge too. One of the actresses thought she was auditioning for a glitzy showbiz extravaganza called 120 Days of **Stardom!** Can you imagine! But I asked them all how they felt about nudity, and they said they'd take their clothes off if the part really demanded it. And I said, well dear, in this show you'll only keep them **on** if the part really demands it. But they're **actors** you know, and maybe I shouldn't really have used actors, I should have simply found some like-minded **people**. Actors are always worried about their next job, they um and ah and have to phone their agents. One has to constantly explain and justify, which is frightfully time-consuming and breaks up the flow. But they all look absolutely divine, they sound wonderful, and they all work so well together.

Q: Mike Tezcan sounds so much like Bela Lugosi, maybe because of his Turkish accent.

NH: He's wonderful, isn't he? Mike is our reference to Hammer Horror! I adore Bela Lugosi (adopts Lugosi accent) - "You vill be locked in da castle until sunrise ..."

Q: How much has that area been an influence to you?

NH: Well, my favourite film actor is Peter Lorre. So you can kind of bridge the gap from there. It's that charismatic ugliness, with the tongue slightly in the cheek. Maybe the play does have a touch of Gothic Horror about it. At the end, there's also a reference to Bunuel's **L'Age d'Or** - the desecration of the religious icon to the 'Descent into Hell' from **Don Giovanni**. But it's also a decadent parody of the end of **Don Giovanni**, where the Don, who's a libertine, goes mad and invites a religious statue to dine with him. So we have the four libertines invite a religious statue to dine with them - on shit from the chamber pots. There are lots of oblique references and cross-references throughout. Someone said the other day "Oh, brilliant -the Kellogg's Cornflakes in the variety pack, good reference!" I said, oh yeah? (laughs) Apparently it had been in one of those 'Did you know?' articles in the papers, that cornflakes had originally been invented - and again it's a repressive Victorian thing - because the properties of corn supposedly suppress the libido. And it was thought that corn first thing in the morning would stop little boys wanking. So of course I said yes, that was deliberate ... (laughs)

Q: **Do you believe that in 120 Days Sade was making a contrived effort to shock even himself?**

NH: Put yourself into his state of mind - behind bars for twenty-seven years, no way of expressing his anger, his sexuality, his imagination. It was said of Aleister Crowley that he had no imagination because he had no repressions; if he felt a desire, he acted upon it immediately. It's equally true that Sade had an excess of imagination and that he spent half his time trying to wind people up - a characteristic some say I share, God forbid! (laughs) But I think if Sade had actually been confronted by some of the delights he concocted, he'd have been appalled. The perverse pleasures and deviations were specifically attributed to his characters, in order to create this political cartoon. He saw how corrupt the Ancien Régime was, and caricatured it, horrifically. That's why they hated him so much!

Q: **How much of the actual philosophy contained in the book have you tried to present in the stage production?**

NH: Because the book is so enormous, in terms of character, event, and in terms of philosophy, it's very diverse and he leads himself up blind alleys at times. But there does seem to be a progressive through-line talking about how escalating depravity can be increasingly exciting. The more awful a crime, the more pleasure it will give. It's almost like the drug thing, you know, each time the kick has to be bigger. I've tried to encapsulate that.

Q: Three hundred pages of filth to a sentence.

NH: (laughs) If you like. But it's not purporting to be a precise adaptation. It's a free, impressionistic version. That's the way it's got to be - unless you do an RSC **Nicholas Nickleby** on it, an eight hour show with a company of sixty. I mean, that would be great, but who would fund it? (laughs)

Q: Do you not feel that, in the jaded perversity of 120 days, Sade was aware of the sometimes ludicrous lengths to which some men must go to achieve orgasm?

NH: Yes ... I ... do ... Sorry, I can't really think of anything else to say about that ...! (laughs)

Q: "When one's prick is aloft, it is horror, villainy, the appalling, that pleases ..." Do you feel that Sade's statement is universal? (No personal prying intended)

NH: There's a lovely American aphorism: "an erect penis has no conscience". Wickedness is certainly a part of what pleases some people. I prefer to commit my crimes on the stage.

Q: Do you see yourself as a vehicle for Sade's philosophy, rather than discussing whether it's good or bad?

NH: The **show** is. **I'm not**, necessarily ...! (laughs) The show is a vehicle for exploring Sade, for presenting his philosophy. He's so frequently taken out of context. The popular misconception is that he's just interested in whipping: if you're a sadist, that means you get a thrill from whipping people. Which is so ridiculous, so absurd. And I think it's a good thing we're at least giving people food for thought, dragging the whole thing out of the closet for discussion.

Q: So you're not trying to convey some deep and meaningful message?

NH: I don't think it's right to hijack a text for didactic ends. Three was a recent theatrical adaptation of **Fanny Hill** where the text had been hijacked for a feminist interpretation. I didn't think it was particularly successful, not very effective at all. All I've tried to do is present Sade truthfully, faithfully. Let others discuss it.

Q: Many regard Sade as the ultimate misogynist. How do you feel, given his characters' joyous disregard for female life, and the preference for the male anus over the vagina?

NH: Any of his biographers tell you he had an extremely healthy interest in women. All the misogyny, all the evil in **120 Days** is assigned to the libertines for the reasons I've already explained. Would Sade have married and conducted a relationship with a mistress had he been a true misogynist? I don't think so.

Q: Taking him out of context again, do you think?

NH: He seems to me, from all I've read about him, from all the diverse material available, to have been a person with an enormous love of life. But there he was, you know, locked away in his prison cell on his own, a man who enjoyed being with people, living life to the full, stirring things up a bit, metaphorically and literally ... All sorts of things are going to come out - in anger, or whatever. No, I don't think Sade was a misogynist. I think he loved women - and men - loved being with people. But hated injustice. It was a difficult position to be in, an aristocrat who hated the aristocracy.

Q: You've avoided the repetition which becomes so wearing, and ultimately nauseating, in the original novel.

NH: It's potted Sade. Chamber-potted. I must confess there's quite a bit of coprophagia, but we largely concentrate on the rituals, the weddings between the prisoners, the deflowerings, the deaths - the more interesting, inherently theatrical material. There are also scenes of psychological torture, such as when the libertines get a kick out of putting a gun in the little girl's mouth. It's structured so that the whole thing becomes progressively horrible. It moves from a basic, deliberately misleading sauciness, becomes unnervingly disgusting, and is finally very horrific. We've kept to Sade's numerical order of events, his pattern of action/anecdote/action, and all his rules for the Chateau de Silling. And there are punishment scenes for transgressing those rules. But there's also an underlying vein of black comedy. Maybe the material is sick, but it's delightfully funny! If it's not taken literally, that is. Lacing the cake, I suppose you could call it, like a wedding cake laced with acid. The humour is there to make the public swallow the really subversive stuff.

Q: **What has been the general press attitude to the show so far?**

NH: Spectacularly divided! Everyone's fascinated by something that seems on the surface to be rather appalling. That's the English all over, isn't it? They like to dip their toes in, like to get their thrills vicariously. But I'm not sure that anyone really knows what to say about it because it doesn't have the familiar construction of a play, there are no real characters, there's no dramatic conflict or psychological revelation. It shares it's episodic, linear progression with Japanese theatre. And of course, when you're dealing with this sort of material, personal taste, personal limits come very much to the fore - what is too much for one person isn't far enough for another. But you expect that. The only thing that really worried me was the call for it to be more erotic. **Erotic?** Cruelty, mutilation, murder?? These people were either revealing their complete ignorance of Sade or telling us something quite disturbing about their own peccadilloes ... perhaps both. But whatever their attitude to the content, all of them say it's a fabulous sensual extravaganza - which, of course, it is!

Q: Having any problems with censorship?

NH: The trouble with the whole Mary Whitehouse mentality is that it takes everything at face value, without benefit of irony or imagination. I suppose if you take passages (forgive the pun) out of context, the explicit nature of the material could be difficult for some to take. I don't know which will give the most offence, the blasphemy or the coprophagia. And all in the Conservative stronghold of Wandsworth! There were a lot of problems before we opened ... one or two people heard that we were planning to gang-bang the Madonna and shit in her mouth for the finale. And again, taken out of context, yes, it's disturbing, but a suitably colossal, cataclysmic ending is required. By that time, the libertines have become almost subhuman. You can't see them as real Judges and Bishops saying that it's a jolly good thing to shit in the mouth of Madonna. Anyway, it's **not** the Madonna, it's a non-specific religious icon. That's what gets you round the law. (laughs) It's a non-specific Greek statue, wearing a nun's habit. I think since people have seen it, they realise we're certainly not promoting anything unpleasant. They appreciate the distancing effect achieved by the humour, the irony, the theatrical stylisation. As I said, it's a portrayal of Sade's philosophy.

Q: **So what do you think of the Moyra Bremner backlash, trying to ban Juliette?**

NH: Upholding complete freedom of speech is ultimately more important than trying to ban one little book. There are far more truly obscene things around after all. As I said, Sade can't operate as erotica or pornography because there's no tease in it. And when you read the books as a whole, it's quite plain that the behaviour is being attacked, not advocated. I guess it's unfortunate that **Justine** was found among Ian Brady's possessions, but I don't think he stood up in court and said "This is why", did he?

Q: **What are your plans for the future? Do you want to make films?**

NH: Of course! I'd love to make a film of this - I wonder if Ken Russell would be interested ...? If not him, I might persuade Disney to make a version of it - **101 Dalmatians of Sodom** perhaps ...? In the very near future, I'm going to form a permanent company, peopled with angels, beauties, extraordinary personalities to breathe life into my fantasies, perhaps a dwarf or two, or siamese twins. It'll be a cross between an Elizabethan company, you know, with its clowns, and an old Victorian travelling circus. We'll roll continually around the globe, leaving an endless trail of glitter and confetti in our wake ... **120 Days** will be in repertoire with my Crowley **Tempest**, the Warhol project I mentioned, and a new thing I'm working on which is a study of Victorian sexuality, Pre-Raphaelite little girls, fairy tales. And I'll want to return to **Lolita** before long. These shows will stay in the repertoire forever, evolving, changing - the challenge is not to perfect (and then endlessly repeat) the **details** of each performance, but to activate the psychic alchemy, the energy-exchange between the performers **and** between the stage and the audience. We have to constantly surprise and enchant each other to be able to have the same effect upon the public. There's a lot of interest in both **120 Days** and **Tempest** overseas, so perhaps I ought to be thinking about renewing my passport quite soon. Ideally, of course, I'd like to be **forced** to leave the country ... it's so romantic, isn't it? My last words will be "Take me to Pere-Lachaise!" So long as they don't put me next to Jim Morrison. You know, I only went to see **The Doors** because I thought it was going to be about Diana Dors ... I can't tell you how disappointed I was.

Q: **I can imagine. Thank you.**

CREATION PRESS / ANNIHILATION PRESS
Autumn 1991 - Spring 1992

"RAISM" James Havoc   IBSN 1 871592 00 3
The controversial hymn to Satanist Gilles de Rais. Illustrated by Jim Navajo, co-founder Primal Scream. "(Havoc) ... is one of the three best poets writing in the English language." - **NME.**
"A madman to watch." - **BLITZ.**   £4.95

"POEMS 1827-49" Edgar Allan Poe   ISBN 1 871592 01 1
A collection of his best poetry, illustrated with lithographs by Odilon Redon.
Creation Classics I   £4.95

"THE BLACK BOOK" Tony Reed (Ed.)   ISBN 1 871592 03 8
Extreme dark fantasy stories by new writers. Illus. "... reminiscent of Roald Dahl after the blast of My Bloody Valentine and some vicious acid" - **CUT.**   £4.95

"BODY BAG" Henry Rollins   ISBN 1 871592 04 6
A brutal collection of works from the American hardcore hero turned literary terrorist.
"A violent odyssey of pain" - **SOUNDS.**   £5.95
REPRINTING MARCH '92.

"THE JACKASS THEORY" Henry Rollins   ISBN 1 871592 05 4
A collection of two books, "Knife Street" and "1,000 Ways to Die", in one volume.   £5.95

"RED HEDZ" Michael Paul Peter   ISBN 1 871592 02 X
Extreme tale of psycho-sexual tyranny and mutation. "... takes writers like William Burroughs and Clive Barker as merely the starting-point for a mixture of poetry, cut-up fiction, hallucinatory rantings and keenly observed characterisation." - **SKELETON CREW**
(The Triple Tease Vol.1)   £5.95

"CATHEDRAL LUNG" Aaron Williamson   ISBN 1 871592 06 2
A volume of ecstatic rage from the eccentric writer and performer, who is also profoundly deaf. "Aaron seems to confront his anger by grabbing language by the throat ... creates something radically different from most writers." - **SOUNDBARRIER.**
"... a furious gnostic prayer ... machine-gunning the page, ricocheting against our smug complacent ears." - **Brian Catling,** *poet.*   £4.95

"CEASE TO EXIST"   ISBN 1 871592 07 0
A Creation Press Sampler. The best from the first two years; includes Henry Rollins, James Havoc.   £4.95

"PHILOSOPHY IN THE BOUDOIR"   The Marquis de Sade
Translated by Meredith Bodroghy   ISBN 1 871592 09 7
De Sade's masterpiece; seven dialogues which fully expound his doctrine of libertinage - a philosophy hailed as the main cornerstone of Surrealism. Modern imagination starts here.
Creation Classics II.   £4.95

"RED STAINS" Jack Hunter (Ed.) ISBN 1 871592 08 9

New stories of extreme biological fantasy and the psycho-sexual imagination. A successor to the "Black Book". Authors include Ramsey Campbell, Jeremy Reed, James Havoc, Michael Paul Peter. (March 1992) £5.95

"SATANSKIN" James Havoc ISBN 1 871592 10 0

Twenty adult fairy-tales of twisted imagination from the young "madman", disclosing an occult world of weird magic, insanity, and bizarre sexuality. The book will also be available in a severely limited edition as a hand-crafted, individually tattooed and numbered skin bible.

(April 1992) £5.95

"RAISM - The Songs of Gilles de Rais"
James Havoc and Mike Philbin
Part One: "Meathook Seed" ISBN 1 871592 16 X

Havoc's infamous anti-novel, heavily edited and revised to form a graphic novel in 3 parts, illustrated by Mike Philbin of "Red Hedz" notoriety. Surreal, explicit; a new classic, unique in its genre. Creation Graphics 1 *(May 1992)* £5.95

"ED GEIN - PSYCHO" Paul A. Woods ISBN 1 871592 21 6

Weird, nightmarish but true story of murder, grave-robbing, mutilation, necrophilia, and cannibalism; the story of the woodsman who turned his lonely farmstead into a slaughterhouse for human cattle. Real-life inspiration for films such as "Psycho" and "The Silence of the Lambs". Includes Gein biography with crime photographs, plus illustrated filmography. Definitive.

(February 1992) £6.95

FOR FURTHER INFORMATION, CONTACT CREATION PRESS (Dept. E), 83 CLERKENWELL ROAD, LONDON EC1. Tel: 071 430 9878

ALL TITLES AVAILABLE BY MAIL ORDER. PLEASE SEND CHEQUES OR POSTAL ORDERS FOR THE STATED AMOUNT, PLUS 75p EACH TITLE, FOR POSTAGE AND PACKING (£1.50 OVERSEAS)

PLEASE SEND A STAMPED, ADDRESSED ENVELOPE FOR OUR 16 PAGE CATALOGUE OF TITLES IN STOCK, AND RELATED MATERIAL